I0202464

Is postcolonial theory bla-boring? A return to primary texts.
Selections from the writings of Raja Rammohun Roy (1772-
1833).

O₂pen Windows: A Feminist Research Center.

Published by

LIES AND BIG FEET

Copyright © 2015. This collection Lies and Big Feet. Readers of these articles may copy them without the copyright owner's permission, if the author and publisher are acknowledged in the copy and copy is used for educational, not-for-profit purposes.

All rights reserved.

ISBN: 9384281093
ISBN-13: 978-9384281090

DEDICATION

IN THE HOPE THAT WE REALISE THAT
POSTCOLONIAL THEORY, AS A LITERARY
MOVEMENT, IS DEAD.

CONTENTS

THE PURPOSE OF THE BOOK.

The first two chapters allow the readers an insight into the socio-cultural context within which Raja Rammohun Roy (1772-1833) was working. The second half of the book contains selections from the works of Rammohun, and each chapter has an introductory note which elaborates an approach on how to interpret his writings.

SECTION I.

1 INTRODUCTION: IS POSTCOLONIAL THEORY BLA-BLA?

Are we eternally condemned to describe the processes of intellectual and technical exchange and engagement that took place between colonizer and colonized/ English and native, within a single interpretative framework: namely, that of postcolonial theory? A lot of this theory operates from the premise that the colonialist, imperial project and its discourses inevitably and always make use of specific fixed ideas to how the native "other" is to be defined: as "heathen, barbarian, chaos, violence".[1] For example, Homi Bhaba, in one of his seminal essays, "Signs Taken for Wonder," draws upon a narrative which describes natives being awe struck at the materiality of the printed book.[2] He argues that the book as used by the natives was a hybrid formation; the "effect of colonial power," he writes, is the "production of hybridisation rather than the noisy command of colonialist authority or silent repression of native tradition."[3] In other words, Bhaba suggests

---

[1] Homi Bhabha, "Sly Civility," in *The Location of Culture* (New York: Routledge, 1994), Reprint 2005, pp. 132-144, p. 143.

[2] Homi Bhabha, "Signs Taken for Wonders: questions of ambivalence and authority under a tree outside Delhi, May 1817" in *The Location of Culture*, pp. 145-174.

[3] Ibid., p. 160.

that the engagement between the colonial powers and the native always results in a hybrid formation.

And so, we ask: what exactly is this notion of the hybrid? Is it a cultural phenomenon, specific to the last few centuries. Helen Tiffin[4] makes such an assumption when she states that postcolonial cultures are "inevitably hybridized, involving a dialectical relationship between European ontology and epistemology and the impulse to create or recreate independent local identity."[5] She goes on to write that decolonization "invokes an ongoing dialectic between hegemonist centrist systems and peripheral subversion of them; between European or British discourses and their post-colonial dis/mantling."[6] Therefore, the project of post-colonial writings is to investigate the means by "which Europe imposed and maintained its codes on the colonial domination of so much of the rest of the world."[7] Tiffin assumes that native cultures were completely overwritten by colonial presence, and that Europeans dictated terms which left little space for natives to maneuver their positions and identities

What we forget is that the natives were negotiating with the European Other, and simultaneously re-examining and rewriting their own epistemic systems. Reading primary texts

---

[4] Helen Tiffin, "Postcolonial Literatures and Counter Cultures," in *The Post-colonial Studies Reader*, ed. Bill Ashcroft, Gareth Griffiths and Helen Tiffin (London: Routledge, 1995), pp. 95-98.

[5] Ibid., p. 95.

[6] Ibid., p. 95.

[7] Ibid., p. 95.

written by natives allows us a completely different perspective on how colonization took place in the last few centuries. Even if we agree that the hegemonic center had cultural supremacy in dictating terms on how the natives were to be portrayed to the world, it would be foolish to assume that the natives were silent spectators. They might have been peripheral in relation to the West, at that moment, but they were quite central within a Self-native perspective. The question therefore is, why should we, at this moment, care as to how the colonizers perceived the natives and instead, our focus should be on how the natives perceived the Self and the colonizer-Other, and in the process, renegotiated with identities of the Self.

One way of doing so would be by examining primary texts and literary works that were written during this time period. And it is keeping this perspective in mind that we examine the writings of Raja Rammohun Roy (1772-1833) and his use of the newly emerged realm of print in colonial Calcutta in the early decades of the nineteenth century; doing so will allow us to conclude that postcolonial theory, as a valid analytical tool, is defunct.

2 RAMMOHUN ROY AND PRINT.

In the newly established realm of print culture set up by the Britishers in the last two decades of the eighteenth century, it did not take long for the natives to pick up the new technology, and the English language. This process of exchange and learning was made possible through close interaction. In fact, within a few decades, native writers in English saw their works being printed in England and reaching out both to a readership in England and India. In 1832, the London publishing house, Smith Elder and Co. published Rammohun Roy's[8] *Exposition of the Practical Operation of the Judicial and Revenue Systems of India and of the General Character and condition of its Native Inhabitants, As submitted in Evidence to the authorities in England.*[9] This work was, in part, a response to certain questions that had been raised in the English Parliament regarding the habits and conditions of India.

What is remarkable in the *Exposition* is Rammohun's thorough

---

[8] Throughout these chapters, I will refer to Rammohun Roy as Rammohun. For his works, I have referred to: *The English Works of Raja Rammohun Roy. Parts I - V*. ed. Dr. Kalidas Nag and Debajyoti Burman (Calcutta: Sadharon Brahmo Samaj, 1948).

[9] Rammohun Roy. *Exposition of the Practical Operation of the Judicial and Revenue Systems of India and of the General Character and condition of its Native Inhabitants, As submitted in Evidence to the authorities in England* (London: Smith Elder, 1832). This was a report that Rammohun Roy submitted to the House of Commons in England in 1831.

understanding of the European systems of political and social thought. Rammohun was largely educated within pre-colonial educational systems, which were uninfluenced by European knowledge. It was only when he started working for different officials of the East India Company from 1805 that he learned about Western systems of thinking. About his education on Western civilization he wrote in the *Exposition*:

> From occasionally directing my studies to the subjects and events peculiarly connected with Europe, and from an attentive though partial, practical observation in regard to some of them, I felt impressed with the idea, that in Europe literature was zealously encouraged and knowledge widely diffused; that mechanics were almost in a state of perfection, and politics in daily progress; ...
>
> I arrived in England on the 8th of April following. The particulars of my voyage and travels will be found in a Journal which I intend to publish.[10]

Here, Rammohun reveals his admiration for all aspects of modern Western civilization; he also reveals an awareness of himself as a public intellectual, operating in a realm of print that traveled within India and the Western worlds. Why was he so keen to write a travelogue of his voyage to England?— Rammohun was fond of print to the point where whatever he thought about and wanted to do found its way into print. Even his theological and social disputes were worked out in print. He reveled in print, dashing off pamphlets to the printers.[11] He

---

[10] Ibid., p.8.

[11] Most moderately wealthy people in Britain made use of print for semi permanent

enjoyed the publicity that his printed works gave him, by reaching a local and a global readership. The realm of English native print in Calcutta in the early nineteenth century was dominated by the writings of Rammohun Roy, but how was it possible for Rammohun to operate within the newly formed communications circuit that specifically targeted the native readers? How did printing take place in Calcutta, and who were involved? How was it possible for native entrepreneurs to pick up the new technology?

New theoretical interventions.

We have a hazy picture of the early years of the "communication circuit" that emerged in Calcutta in the 1780s. We find Hindu natives rubbing shoulders with the Europeans as they joined labor in setting up print foundries and presses, and a new city was established with all the paraphernalia of European civilization—many natives were going to eventually be "suited" and "booted." Ships arrived at the docks loaded with books, consumer items for the colonizers, and a whole lot of material for printing presses; it also came loaded with men who brought intellectual labour. Alongside Hindu and Islamic cultures, a new civilization emerged in India. How do we account for this degree of pluralism and multi-culturalism? I am immediately drawn to Paul Gilroy's theoretical position in *The Black Atlantic as a Counterculture of Modernity*, where he argues against nationalist or ethnically absolute identities, specifically

---

documents and official correspondence, legal notices, circulars, etc. Some still used scribes. Rammohun's use of print in this manner is clearly a Western habit, which he must have picked up as a result of his interaction with the officials of the Company for whom he worked.

the English nation state which defines itself as "ceaselessly" giving birth to itself, "seemingly from Britannia's head."[12] Gilroy draws attention to the possibility of a transnational and transcultural perspective—the Atlantic, which gave birth to the black diaspora, can affect how we view the western hemisphere, and concepts of ethnic authenticity. As Gilroy argues, one needs double consciousness in order to be both "European and black,"[13] like the numerous travelers and exiles like William Du Bois, Richard Wright and Martin Robison Delaney. Ships moving between nations, "crossing borders in modern machines" were "micro systems of linguistic and political hybridity."[14] The western artistic imagination of the eighteenth century was replete with icons of the ship, or the slave ship; "ships were the living means by which the points within that Atlantic world were joined."[15]

News of sailing ships was an important and regular feature in the Indian newspapers that were printed in the last two decades of the eighteenth century. Ships were the most important links between the colonies and the metropole; Most importantly, ships carried more than goods and news—they carried people who started British establishments that were more than trading enclaves in different parts of India. Thereby, the whole of Indian society underwent gradual changes, adding a European identity to the existing Islamic and Hindu ones. Such a

---

[12] Paul Gilroy, *The Black Atlantic: Modernity and Double Consciousness* (London, Verso, 1993), p.14.

[13] Ibid., p. 1.

[14] Ibid., p. 12.

[15] Ibid., p. 16.

perspective allows us to look at the processes of colonialism from a global angle. We can disregard the fact that the natives had little agency in determining how they were perceived by the hegemonic Center who often represented them within binaries of colonized-Other, but we should not turn a myopic eye to the fact that the natives were negotiating with the new-ness of western civilization in ways that benefited them. Reading primary texts allows us an insight in understanding the nature of this epistemic shift that was being made.

SECTION II:
READING PRIMARY TEXTS.

3 EXTRACTS FROM THE BRAHMANICAL MAGAZINE (1821).

Even before settling in Calcutta in 1814, Rammohun was not innocent of the nature of printed texts. It is safe to assume that even though his education in his early years would have primarily made use of manuscripts, by the time he was working in 1805 for different officials of the East India Company, he would have also become familiar with printed books and journals, particularly as, in these days before typewriting, most Government circulars and notices were printed. Nonetheless, it was only after he moved to Calcutta in 1814 that he gained access to the technology of print and started publishing his works; *Vedanta Grantha* (1815) and *Vedanta Sastra* (1815) were his first printed texts. These works were printed privately and were in Bengali. In many ways, what distinguishes Rammohun from his native contemporaries, who also were participating in the newly established realm of print, is his hyper-critical awareness of the characteristics of print—that mechanically reproduced printed texts could reach across to a large reading audience. While at Rangpur, in north Bengal, working for John Digby, he had familiarized himself with European political developments by reading English newspapers and journals that were subscribed to by Digby. Rammohun knew that the texts that he read would have traveled a great distance from their original place of publication in England. This fact would not have been lost on Rammohun, which made Calcutta, with its nascent print industry, an attractive city to him. He realized that he could make use of print technology to become a political and intellectual participant in the new British regime in Calcutta. Amongst the native intelligentsia of this time, Rammohun was unique as he could understand and comprehend the extent to which print worked.

THE BRAHMUNICAL MAGAZINE OR THE MISSIONARY AND THE BRAHMUN BEING A VINDICATION OF THE HINDOO RELIGION AGAINST THE ATTACKS OF CHRISTIAN MISSIONARIES.
CALCUTTA,
1821.

PREFACE TO THE FIRST EDITION.

For a period of upwards of fifty years, this country (Bengal) has been in exclusive possession of the English nation; during the first thirty years of which, from their word and deed, it was universally believed that they would not interfere with the religion of their subjects, and that they truly wished every man to act in such matters according to the dictates of his own conscience. Their possessions in Hindoostan and their political strength have, through the grace of God gradually increased. But during the last twenty years, a body of English gentlemen who are called missionaries, have been publicly endeavouring, in several ways, to convert Hindoos and Mussulmans of this country into Christianity. The first way is that of publishing and distributing among the natives various books, large and small, reviling both religions, and abusing and ridiculing the gods and saints of the former: the second way is that of standing in front of the doors of the natives or in the public roads to preach the excellency of their own religion and the debasedness of that of others: the third way is that if any natives of low origin become Christians from the desire of gain or from any other motives, these gentlemen employ and maintain them as a necessary encouragement to others to follow their example.

It is true that the apostles of Jesus Christ used to preach the superiority of the Christian religion to the natives of different countries. But we must recollect that they were not of the rulers of those countries where they preached. Were the missionaries likewise to preach the Gospel and distribute books in countries not conquered by the English, such as Turkey, Persia, &c., which are such nearer England, they would be esteemed a body of men truly zealous in propagating their religion and in following the example of the founders of Christianity. In Bengal, where the English are the sole rulers, and where the mere name of Englishman is sufficient to frighten people, an encroachment upon the rights of her poor timid and humble inhabitants and upon their religion, cannot be viewed in the eyes of God or the public as a justifiable act. For wise and good men always feel disinclined to hurt those that are of much less strength than themselves, and if such
weak creatures be dependent on them and subject to their authority, they can never attempt, even in thought, to mortify their feelings.

We have been subjected to such insults for about nine centuries, and the cause of such degradation has been our excess in civilization and abstinence from the slaughter even of animals;

as well as our division into castes, which has been the source of want of unity among us.

It seems almost natural that when one nation succeeds in conquering another, the former, though their religion may be quite ridiculous, laugh at and despise the religion and manners of those that are fallen into their power. For example, Mussulmans, upon their conquest of India, proved highly inimical to the religious exercises of Hindoos. When the generals of Chungezkhan, who denied God and were like wild beasts in their manners, invaded the western part of Hindoostan, they universally mocked at the profession of God and of futurity expressed to them by the natives of India. The savages of Arracan, on their invasion of the eastern part of Bengal, always attempted to degrade the religion of Hindoos. In ancient days, the Greeks and the Romans, who were gross idolators and immoral in their lives, used to laugh at the religion and conduct of their Jewish subjects, a sect who were devoted to the belief of one God. It is therefore not uncommon if the English missionaries, who are of the conquerors of this country, revile and mock at the religion of its natives. But as the English are celebrated for the manifestation of humanity and for administering justice, and as a great many gentlemen among them are noticed to have had an aversion to violate equity, it would tend to destroy their acknowledged character if they follow the example of the former savage conquerors in disturbing the established religion of the country; because to introduce a religion by means of abuse and insult, or by affording the hope of worldly gain, is inconsistent with reason and justice. If by the force of argument they can prove the truth of their own religion and the falsity of that of Hindoos, many would of course embrace their doctrines, and in case they fail to prove this, they should not undergo such useless trouble, nor tease Hindoos any longer by their attempts at conversion. In consideration of the small huts in which Brahmuns of learning generally reside, and the simple food, such as vegetables &c., which they are accustomed to eat, and the poverty which obliges them to live upon charity, the missionary gentlemen may not, I hope, abstain from controversy from contempt of them, for truth and true religion do not always belong to -wealth and power, high names, or lofty palaces.

Now, in the Mission-press of Shreerampore a letter showing the unreasonableness of all the Hindoo Shastrus having appeared, I have inserted in the 1st and 2nd number of this magazine all the questions in the above letter as well as their answers, and afterwards the replies that may be made by both parties shall in like manner be published.

PREFACE TO THE SECOND EDITION.

In giving the contents of the following pages to the world in a new edition, I think it necessary to prefix a short explanation of the origin of the controversy, and the manner in which it concluded. The BRAHMUNICAL MAGAZINE was commenced for the purpose of answering the objections against the Hindoo Religion contained in a Bengallee Weekly Newspaper, entitled "SUMMACHAR DURPUN," conducted by some of the most eminent of the Christian Missionaries, and published at Shreerampore. In that paper of the 14th July, 1821, a letter was inserted containing certain doubts regarding the Shastrus, to which the writer invited any one to favour him with an answer, through the same channel. I accordingly sent a reply in the Bengallee language, to which, however, the conductors of the work calling for it, refused insertion; and I therefore formed the resolution of publishing the whole controversy with an English translation in a work of my own "the Brahmunical Magazine," now re-printed, which contains all that was written on both sides.

In the first number of the MAGAZINE I replied to the arguments they adduced against the Shastrus, or immediate explanations of the Veds, our original Sacred Books; and in the second I answered the objections urged against the Poorans and Tantras, or Historical Illustrations of the Hindoo Mythology, showing that the doctrines of the former are much more rational than the religion which the Missionaries profess, and that those of the latter, if unreasonable, are not more so than their Christian Faith. To this the Missionaries made a reply in their work entitled the "FRIEND OF INDIA," No. 38, which was immediately answered by me in the 3rd No. of the Magazine; and from the continuation of a regular controversy of this kind, I expected that in a very short time, the truth or fallacy of one or other of our religious systems would be clearly established; but to my great surprise and disappointment, the Christian Missionaries, after having provoked the discussion, suddenly abandoned it; and the 3rd No. of my Magazine has remained unanswered for nearly two years. During that long period the Hindoo community, (to whom the work was particularly addressed and therefore printed both in Bengallee and English), have made up their minds that the arguments of the BRAHMUNICAL MAGAZINE are unanswerable; and I now republish, therefore, only the English translation, that the learned among Christians, in Europe as well as in Asia, may form their opinion on the subject.

It is well-known to the whole world, that no people on earth are more tolerant than the Hindoos, who believe all men to be equally within the reach of Divine beneficence, which embraces the good of every religious sect and denomination: therefore it cannot be imagined that my object in publishing this Magazine was to oppose Christianity; but I was influenced by the conviction that persons who travel to a distant country for the purpose of overturning the opinions of its inhabitants and introducing their own, ought to be prepared to demonstrate that the latter are more reasonable than the former.

In conclusion, I beg to ask every candid and reflecting reader: Whether a man be placed on an imperial throne, or sit in the dust whether he be lord of the whole known world, or destitute of even a hut the commander of millions, or without a single follower whether he be intimately acquainted with all human learning, or ignorant of letters whether he be ruddy and handsome, or dark and deformed yet if while he declares that God is not man, he again professes to believe in a God-Man or Man-God, under whatever sophistry the idea may be sheltered, can such a person have a just claim to enjoy respect in the intellectual world? and does he not expose himself to censure, should he, at the same time, ascribe unreasonableness to others?

4 A DEFENCE OF HINDOO THEISM (1817).

Rammohun's Vedantic works can be described as the first
Vedantic commentaries in a vernacular that were written for a
non-Hindu, non-Sanskrit speaking readership.[16] He was aware
of this as he draws attention to this fact in *A Defence of Hindoo
Theism*, "I must remark, however, that there is no translation of
the Vedas into any of the modern languages of Hindoostan with
which I am acquainted."[17] His works are exegeses on the
commentaries of Shankaracharya and have a precedence in
Baladeva Bidyabhusan's *Govindabhasya* and *Isabhasya*, which were
the first Bengali commentaries that were written in the
eighteenth century. The only exception was Dara Shukoh's
translations two hundred years ago around 1641. Dara Shukoh
was the oldest son of Jahangir, and attracted a liberal courtly
crowd of scholars, imperial officers and nobles who followed
the eclectic ideology of Akbar. He was a follower of Mullah Mir
(d. 1635) and Mullah Shah Badeshi (d. 1661), two important
Sufi teachers. He was firmly convinced that the Upanishads
preached monotheism, in a similar fashion as did Islam. With
the help of Brahmin scholars whom he invited from Benares, he

---

[16] For more see Bruce Carlisle Robertson, *Raja Rammohun Roy. The Father of Modern
India.* (Delhi: Oxford University Press, 1999), pp. 30-31.

[17] *A Defence of Hindoo Theism. In Reply to the Attack of an Advocate for Idolatory in Madras.
1817.* In *The English Works of Raja Rammohun Roy. Part II*, p. 85.

translated fifty two Upanishads and titled the work *Sirr-i-Akbar*. In 1671, a French traveler to India named Francis Bernier returned to France with a copy of the Persian *Upanishads*, which were translated into Latin by Duperron and titled *Oupnek'hat*. It is not clear if William Jones knew this work when he, with his group of Benares *pandits*, translated the *Isa Upanishads* in 1799. He was assisted in his works by Hindu *pandits*, but none of their names are featured in the published works. In the early years of the nineteenth century, Rammohun, as a result of his familiarity with the officials of the East India Company and the Baptist missionaries, would have known about the works of William Jones and his collaborative use of pandits.[18] The reading domain within which Rammohun worked was already inhabited by European Orientalist scholars. It is almost as if Rammohun was challenging these scholars and their lack of acknowledgement of native support. His readers were the same as those of the Orientalist scholars. Here was an instance of a *pandit* who had turned Orientalist scholar.

A DEFENCE OF HINDOO THEISM (1817)

BEFORE I attempt to reply to the observations that the learned gentleman, who signs himself Sankara Sastri, has offered in his letter of the 26th December last, addressed to the

---

[18] See Robertson's *Raja Rammohun Ray* for more on this; pp. 10-54.

Editor of the *Madras Courier*, on the subject of an article published in the *Calcutta Gazette*, and on my translation of an abridgment of the Vedanta and of the two chapters of the Vedas, I beg to be allowed to express the disappointment I have felt in receiving from a learned Brahman controversial remark, on Hindoo Theology written in a foreign language, as it is the invariable practice of the natives of all provinces of Hindoostan to hold their discussions on such subjects in Sanskrit, which is the learned language common to all of them, and in which they may naturally be expected to convey their ideas with perfect correctness, and greater facility than in any foreign tongue: nor need it be alleged that, by adopting this established channel of controversy, the opportunity of appealing to public opinion on the subject must be lost, as a subsequent translation from the Sanskrit into English may sufficiently serve that purpose. The irregularity of this mode of proceeding, however, gives me room to suspect that the letter in question is the production of the pen of an English gentleman, whose liberality, *I suppose*, has induced him to attempt an apology even for the absurd idolatry of his fellow-creatures. If this inference be correct, while I congratulate that gentleman on his progress in a knowledge of the sublime doctrines of the Vedanta, I must, at the same time, take the liberty of entreating that he will, for the future prefer consulting the original works written upon those doctrines, to relying on the second-hand information on the subject, that may be offered him by any person whatsoever.

The learned gentleman commences by objecting to the terms *discoverer* and *reformer*, in which the Editor of the *Calcutta Gazette*, was pleased to make mention of me. He states, "That people of limited understanding, not being able to comprehend the system of worshipping the invisible Being, have adopted false doctrines, and by that means confounded weak minds in remote times; but due punishment was inflicted on those heretics, and religion was very well established throughout India by the Reverend Sankaracharya and his disciples, who, however, did not pretend to *reform* or *discover* them, or assume the title of a *reformer* or *discoverer.*"

In none of my writings, nor in any verbal discussion, have I ever pretended to reform or to discover the doctrines of the unity God, nor have I ever assumed the title of reformer or discoverer; so far from such an assumption, I have urged in every work that I have hitherto published, that the doctrines of the unity of God are real Hindooism, as that religion was practised by our ancestors, and as it is well-known even at the present age to many earned Brahmans: I beg to repeat a few of the passages to which I allude.

In the introduction to the abridgement of the Vedanta I have said "In order, therefore, to vindicate my own faith and that of our *forefathers*, I have been endeavouring, for some time past, to convince my countrymen of the *true meaning of our sacred* books, and prove that my aberration deserves not the opprobrium which some unreflecting persons have been so ready to throw upon me." In another place of the same introduction: "The present is an endeavour to render an abridgment of the same (the Vedanta) into English, by which I expect to prove to my European friends, that the superstitious practices which deform the Hindoo religion, have nothing to do with the pure spirit of its dictates." In the introduction of the Kenopanishad: "This work will, I trust, by explaining to my countrymen *the real spirit of the Hindoo scriptures which is but the declaration of the unity of God*, tend in a great degree to correct the erroneous conceptions which have Prevailed when regard to the doctrines they inculcate:" and in the Preface of the Isopanishad: "*Many learned Brahmans* are perfectly aware, of the absurdity of idol-worship, and *are well informed of the nature of the "pure mode of divine worship.*" A reconsideration of these passages will, I hope, convince the learned gentleman, that I never advanced any claim to the title either of a reformer or of a discoverer of the doctrines of the unity of the Godhead. It is not at all impossible that from the perusal of the translations above alluded to, the Editor of the *Calcutta Gazette*, finding the system of idolatry into which Hindoos are now completely sunk, quite inconsistent with the real spirit of their scriptures, may have imagined that their contents bad become entirely forgotten and unknown ; and that I was the first to point out the absurdity of idol-,worship, and to inculcate the propriety of the pure divine worship, ordained by their Vedas, their Smritis, and their Puranas. From this idea, and from finding in his intercourse with other Hindoos, that I was stigmatized by many, however unjustly, as an *innovator*, he may have been, not unnaturally, misled to apply to me the epithets of discoverer and reformer.

2ndly. The learned gentleman states: "There are an immense number of books, namely, Vedas, Sastras, Puranas, Agams, Tantras, Sutras, and Itihas, besides numerous commentaries, compiled by many famous theologians, both of ancient and modern times, respecting the doctrines of the worship of the invisible Being. They are not only written in Sanskrit, but rendered into the Prakrita, Telugu, Tamil, Gujrati, Hindoostani, Marhatti, and Canari languages, and immemorially studied by a great part of the Hindu nation, attached to the attached to the adwitam faith, &c." This statement of the learned gentleman, as far as it is correct, corroborates indeed my assertion with respect to the doctrines of the worship of the invisible Supreme Spirit being unanimously inculcated by all the Hindoo Sastras, and naturally leads to severe reflections on the selfishness which must actuate those Brahmanical teachers who, notwithstanding the unanimous authority of the Sastras for the adoption of pure worship, yet, with the view of maintaining the title of God which they arrogate to themselves and of deriving pecuniary and other advantages from the numerous rites and festivals of idol -worship, constantly advance and encourage idolatry to the utmost of their power. I must remark, however, that there is no translation of the Vedas into any of the modern languages of Hindoostan with which I am acquainted, and it is for that reason that I have translated into Bengali the Vedanta, the Kenopanishad of the Sama Veda, the Isopanishad of the Yajur Veda, &c., with the contents of which none but the learned among my countrymen were at all acquainted.

3rdly. The learned gentleman states, that the translations of the scripture into the vulgar language are rejected by some people; and he assigns as reasons for their so doing, that "if the reader of them doubts the truth of the principles explained in the translation the divine knowledge he acquired by them becomes a doubtful faith, and that doubt cannot be removed unless he compare them with the original work: in that case, the knowledge he lastly acquired becomes comes superior, and his study, in the first instance, becomes useless and the cause of repeating the same work." When a translation of a work written in a foreign tongue is made by a person at all acquainted with that language into his native tongue, and the same translation is sanctioned and approved of by many natives of the same country, who are perfectly conversant with that foreign language, the translation, I presume, may be received with confidence as a satisfactory interpretation of the original work, both by the vulgar and by men of literature.

It must not be supposed, however, that I am inclined to assert that there is not the least room to doubt the accuracy of such a translation; because the meaning of authors, even in the original works, is very frequently dubious, especially in a language like Sanskrit, every sentence of which, almost, admits of being explained in different senses. But should the possibility of errors in every translation be admitted as reason for withholding all confidence in their contents, such a rule would shake our belief, not only in the principles explained in the translation of the Vedanta into the current language, but also in all information respecting foreign history and theology obtained by means of translations: in that case, we must either learn all the languages that are spoken by the different nations in the world, to acquire a knowledge of their histories and religions, or be content to know nothing of any country besides our own. The second reason which the learned gentleman assigns for their objection to the translation is that "Reading the scripture in the vulgar languages is prohibited by the Puranas." I have not yet met with any text of any Puranas which prohibit the explanation of the scripture in the vulgar tongue; on the contrary, the Paranas allow that practice very frequently I repeat one of these declarations from the Siva Dharma, quoted by the great Raghunandana. " He who can interpret, according to the ratio of the understanding of his pupils, through Sanskrit, or through the vulgar languages, or by means of the current language of the country, is entitled, spiritual father." Moreover, in every part of Hindoostan all professors of the Sanskrit language instructing beginners in the Vedas, Puranas, and in other Sastras, interpret them in the vulgar languages; especially spiritual fathers in the exposition of those parts of the Vedas and Puranas, which allegorically introduce a plurality of gods and idol-worship, doctrines which tend so much to their own worldly advantage.

The learned gentleman states, that "The first part of the Veda prescribes the mode of performing *yagam* or sacrifice, bestowing *danam* or alms; treats of penance, fasting, and, of worshipping the incarnations, in which the Supreme Deity has appeared on the earth for divine, purposes. The ceremonies performed according to these modes, forsaking their fruits, are affirmed by the Vedas to be mental exercises and mental purifications necessary to obtain the knowledge of the divine nature." I, in common with the Vedas and the Vedanta, and Manu (the first and best of Hindoo lawgivers) as well as with the most celebrated Sankaracharya, deny these ceremonies being necessary to obtain the knowledge of the divine nature, as the Vedanta positively declares, in text 36, section 4th, chapter 3rd: " Man may acquire the true knowledge of God, even without observing the rules and rites prescribed by the Veda for each class: as it is found in the Veda that many persons who neglected the performance of the rites and ceremonies, owing to their perpetual attention to the adoration of the Supreme Being, acquired the true knowledge respecting the Supreme Spirit." The Veda says; "Many learned true believers never worshipped fire, or any celestial gods through fire." And also the Vedanta asserts, in the 1st text of the 3rd section of the 3rd chapter: The worship authorized by all the Vedas is one, as the directions for the worship of the only Supreme Being are invariably found in the Veda, and the epithets of the Supreme, and Omnipresent Being, &c., commonly imply God alone." Manu, as I have elsewhere quoted, thus declares on the same point, chapter 12th, text 92nd: "Thus must the chief of the twice-born, though he neglect the ceremonial rites mentioned in the Sastra, be diligent in attaining a knowledge of God, in controlling his organs of sense, and in repeating the Veda." Again, chapter 4th, text 23rd: "Some constantly sacrifice their breath in their speech, *when they instruct others of God aloud*, and their speech in their breath, *when they meditate in silence*; perceiving in their speech and breath thus employed, the imperishable fruit of a sacrificial offering." 24th: "Other Brahmans incessantly perform those sacrifices only, seeing with the eye of divine learning, that the scriptural knowledge is the root of every ceremonial observance." And also the same author declares in chapter 2nd, text 84 : "All rites ordained in the Veda, oblations to fire gland solemn sacrifices, pass away; but that which passes not away is declared to be the syllable Om, thence called Akshara since it is a symbol of God, the Lord of created beings."

5thly. The learned gentleman states, that "the difficulty of attaining a knowledge of the Invisible and Almighty Spirit is evident from the preceding verses." I agree with him in that point, that the attainment of perfect knowledge of the nature of the God-head is certainly difficult, or rather impossible; but to read the existence of the Almighty Being in his works of nature, is not, I will dare to say, so difficult to the mind of a man possessed of common sense, and unfettered by prejudice, as to conceive artificial images to be possessed, at once, of the opposite natures of human and divine beings, which idolaters constantly ascribe to their idols, strangely believing that things so *constructed* can be converted by ceremonies into *constructors* of the universe.

6thly. The learned gentleman objects to our introducing songs, although expressing only the peculiar tenets of monotheism, and says: "But the holding of meetings, playing music, singing songs, and dancing, which are ranked among carnal pleasures, are not ordained by scripture, as mental purification." The practice of dancing in divine worship, I agree, is not ordained by the scripture, and accordingly never was introduced in our worship; any mention of dancing in the *Calcutta Gazette* must, therefore, have proceeded from misinformation of the Editor. But respecting the propriety of introducing monotheistical songs in the divine worship, I beg leave to refer the gentleman to texts 114th and 115th of the 3rd chapter of Yajnavalkya, who authorizes not only scriptural music in divine contemplation, but also the songs that are composed by the vulgar. It is also evident that any interesting idea is calculated to make more impression upon the mind, when conveyed in musical verses, than when delivered in the form of common conversation.

7thly. The learned gentleman says: "All the Brahmans in this peninsula are studying the same Vedam as are read in the other parts of the country; but I do not recollect to have read or heard of one treating on astronomy, medicine, or arms: the first is indeed an angam of the Vedam, but the two latter are taught in separate Sastras."—in answer to which I beg to be allowed to refer the gentleman to the following text of the Nirvana: "The Vedas, while talking of planets, botany, austere duties, arms, rites, natural consequences, and several other subjects, are purified by the inculcation of the doctrines of the Supreme Spirit." And also to the latter end of the Mahanirvana agam.

From the perusal of these texts, I trust, he will be convinced that the Vedas not only treat of astronomy, medicine, and arms, but also of morality and natural philosophy, and that all arts and sciences that are treated of in other Sastras, were originally introduced by the Vedas: see also Manu, chapter 12, verses 97 and 98. I cannot of course be expected to be answerable for Brahmans neglecting entirely the study of the scientific parts of the Veda, and putting in practice, and promulgating to the utmost of their power, that part of them which, treating of rites and festivals, is justly considered as the source of their worldly advantages and support of their alleged divinity.

8thly. I observe, that on the following statement in my Introduction to the Kenoopanishdad, *viz.*, "Should this explanation given by the Veda itself, as well as by its celebrated commentator, Vyasa, not be allowed to reconcile those passages winch are seemingly at variance with each other, as those that declare the unity of the invisible Supreme Being, with others which describe a plurality of independent visible gods, the whole work must, I am afraid, not only be stripped of its authority, but looked upon as altogether unintelligible," the learned gentleman has remarked that "To say the least of this passage, RAM MOHUN ROY appears quite as willing to abandon as to defend the Scripture of his Religion."

In the foregoing paragraph, however, I did no more than logically confine the case to two points, *viz.*, that the explanation of the Veda and of its commentators must either be admitted as sufficiently reconciling the apparent contradictions between different passages of the Veda or must not be admitted. In the latter case, the Veda must necessarily be supposed to be inconsistent with itself, and therefore altogether unintelligible, which is directly contrary to the faith of Hindus of every description; consequently they must admit that those explanations do sufficiently reconcile the seeming contradictions between the chapters of the Vedas.

9thly. The learned gentleman says that "Their (the attributes and incarnations) worship under various representations, by means of consecrated objects, is prescribed by the scripture to the human race, by way of mental exercises," &c. I cannot admit that the worship of these attributes under various representations, by means of consecrated objects, has been prescribed by the Veda to the HUMAN RACE; as this kind of worship of consecrated objects is enjoined by the Sastra to those only who are incapable of raising their minds to the notion of an invisible Supreme Being. I have quoted several authorities for this assertion in my Preface to the Isopanishad, and beg to repeat here one or two of them: "The vulgar look for their God in water; men of more extended knowledge in celestial bodies; the ignorant in wood, bricks, and stones; but learned men in the Universal Soul. Thus corresponding to the nature of different powers or qualities, numerous figures have been invented for the benefit of those *who are not possessed of sufficient understanding*." Permit me in this instance to ask, whether every Mussulman in Turkey and Arabia, from the highest to the lowest, every Protestant Christian at least of Europe, and many followers of Kabir and Nanak, do worship God without the assistance of consecrated objects? If so, how can we suppose that the human race is not capable of adoring the Supreme Being without the puerile practice of having recourse to visible objects?

10thly. The learned gentleman is of opinion that the attributes of God exist distinctly from God and he compares the relation between God and these attributes to that of a king to his ministers, he says: "If a person be desirous to visit an earthly prince, he ought to be introduced in the first instance by his ministers," &c.; and "in like manner the grace of God ought to be obtained by the grace through the worship of his attributes." This opinion, I am extremely sorry to find, is directly contrary to all the Vedanta doctrines interpreted, to us by the most revered Sankaracharya, which are real adwaita or non-duality; they affirm that God has no second that may be possessed of eternal existence, either of the same nature with himself or of a different nature from him, nor any second of that nature that might be called either his part or his *quality*. The 16th text of the 2nd section of the 3rd chapter: " The Veda has declared the Supreme Being to be mere understanding." The Veda says; "God is real existence, wisdom and eternity." The Veda very often calls the Supreme Existence by the epithets of Existent, Wise, and Eternal; and assigns as the reason for adopting such epithets, that the Veda in the first instance speaks of God according to the human idea, which views quality separately from person, in order to facilitate our Comprehension of objects. In case these attributes should be supposed, as the learned gentleman asserts, to be separate existences, it necessarily follows, that they must be either eternal or non-eternal. The former case, *viz.* the existence of a plurality of beings imbued like God himself with the property of eternal duration, strikes immediately at the root of all the doctrines relative to the unity of the Supreme Being contained in the Vedanta. By the latter sentiment, namely, that the power and attributes of God are not eternal, we are led at once into the belief that the nature of God is susceptible of change, and consequently that He is not eternal, which makes no inconsiderable step towards atheism itself. These are the obvious and dangerous consequences, resulting from the learned gentleman's doctrine that the attributes of the Supreme Being are distinct existences. I am quite at a loss to know how these attributes of the pure and perfect Supreme Being (as the learned gentleman declares them to exist really and separately, and not fictitiously and allegorically,) can be so sensual and destitute of morality as the creating attribute or Brahma is said to be by the Puranas, which represent him in one instance as attempting to commit a rape upon his own daughter. The protecting attribute, or Vishnu, is in another place affirmed to have fraudulently violated the chastity of Brinda, in order to kill her husband. Siva, the new destroying attribute, is said to have had a criminal attachment to Mohini disregarding all ideas of decency. And a thousand similar examples must be familiar to every reader of the Edranas. I should be obliged by the learned gentleman's showing how the contemplation of such circumstances, which are constantly related by the worshippers of these attributes, even in their sermons, can be instrumental towards the purification of the mind, conducive to morality, and productive of eternal beatitude. Besides, though the learned gentleman in this instance considers these attributes to be separate existences, yet in another place he seems to view them as parts of the Supreme Being as he says "If one part of the ocean can be adored the ocean is adored." I am somewhat at a loss to understand how the learned gentleman proposes to reconcile this apparent contradiction. I must observe, however, in this place, that the comparison drawn between the relation of God and those attributes, and that of a king and his minister, totally inconsistent with the faith entertained by Hindoos of the present day; who, so far from considering these objects of worship as mere instruments by which they may arrive at the power of contemplating the God of nature, regard them in the light of independent gods, to whom, however absurdly, they attribute almighty power, and claim to worship, solely on his own account.

11thly. The learned gentleman is dissatisfied with the objection mentioned in my translation, and remarks, that "the objections to worshipping the attributes are not satisfactorily stated by the author." I consequently repeat the following authorities, which I hope may answer my purpose. The following are the declarations of the Veda; "He who worships any God excepting the Supreme Being, and thinks that he himself is distinct and inferior to that God, knows nothing, and is considered as a domestic beast of these gods. A state even so high as that of Brahman does not afford real bliss. Adore God alone. None but the Supreme Being is to be worshipped; nothing excepting him should be adored by a wise man." I repeat also the following text of the Vedanta: "The declaration of the Veda, that those that worship the celestial gods are the food of such gods, is an allegorical expression, and only means, that they are comforts to the Supreme Being is rendered subjects to these gods. The Veda affirms the same."

And the revered Sankaracharya has frequently declared the state of celestial gods to be that of demons, in the Bhashya of the Isopanishad and of others.

To these authorities a thousand other might be added. But should the learned gentleman required some practical grounds for objecting to the idolatrous worship of the Hindoos, I can be at no loss to give him numberless instances, where the ceremonies that have been instituted under the pretext of honouring the all-perfect Author of Nature, are of a tendency utterly subversive of every moral principle.

I begin with Krishna as the most adored of the incarnations, the number of whose devotees is exceedingly great. His worship is made to consist in the institution of his image or picture, accompanied by one or more females, and in the contemplation of his history and behaviour, such as his perpetration of murder upon a female of the name of Putana; his compelling a great number of married and unmarried women to stand before him denuded; his debauching them and several others, to the mortal affliction of their husbands and relations; his annoying them, by violating the laws of cleanliness and other facts of the same nature. The grossness of his worship does not find a limit here. His devotees very often personify (in the same manner as European actors upon stages do) him and his female companions, dancing, with indecent gestures, and singing songs relative to his love and debaucheries. It is impossible to explain in language fit to meet the public eye, the mode in which Mahadeva, or the destroying attributes is worshipped by the generality of the Hindoos suffice it to say, that it is altogether congenial with the indecent nature of the image, under whose form he is most commonly adored.

The stories respecting him which are read by his devotees in the Tantras, are of a nature that, if told of any man, would be offensive to the ears of the most abandoned of either sex. In the worship of Kali, human sacrifices, the use of wine, criminal intercourse and licentious songs are included: the first of these practices has become generally extinct; but it is believed that there are parts of the country where human victims are still offered.

Debauchery, however, universally forms the principal part of the worship of her followers. Nigam and other Tantras may satisfy every reader of the horrible tenets of the worshippers of the two latter deities. The modes of worship of almost all the inferior deities are pretty much the same. Having so far explained the nature of worship adopted by Hindoos in general, for the propitiation of their allegorical attributes, in direct opposition to the mode of pure divine worship inculcated by the Vedas, I cannot but entertain a strong hope that the learned gentleman, who ranks even monotheistical songs among carnal pleasures, and consequently rejects their admittance in worship, will no longer stand forward as an advocate for the worship of separate and independent attributes and incarnations.

12thly. The learned gentleman says, "that the Saviour," meaning Christ, "should be considered a personification of the mercy and kindness of God (I mean actual not allegorical personification)." From the little knowledge I had acquired of the tenets of Christians and those of anti-Christians, I thought there were only three prevailing opinions respecting the nature of Christ. *viz.*. that he was considered by some as the expounder of the laws of God, and the mediator between God and man; by many to be one of the three mysterious persons of the Godhead; whilst others, such as the Jews, say that he was a mere man. But to consider Christ as a personification of the mercy of God is, if I mistake not, a new doctrine in Christianity, the discussion of which, however, has no connection with the present subject. I, however, must observe that this opinion, which the learned gentleman has formed of Christ being a personification of the mercy of God, is similar to that entertained by Mussulmans, for a period of upwards of a thousand years, respecting Mohummud, whom they call the mercy of God upon all his creatures. The learned gentleman, in the conclusion of his observations, has left, as he says, the doctrines of pure allegory to me. It would have been more consistent with justice had he left pure allegory also to the Vedas, which declare, "appellations and figures of all kinds are innovations," and which have allegorically represented God in the figure of the universe: "Fire is his head, the sun and the moon are his two eyes," &c.; and which have also represented all human internal qualities by different earthly objects; and also to Vedas who has strictly followed the Vedas in these figurative representations, and to Sankaracharya, who also adopted the mode of allegory in his Bhashya of the Vedanta and of the Upanishads.

5 A VINDICATION OF THE INCARNATION OF THE DEITY (1823).

It was an extremely small realm of print, where Englishmen and natives involved in the production of knowledge, and in the technology of print, knew each other. The same metallurgists and printers were involved in different printing houses. For example, Bengali letterpress technology was transferred from the East India Company to the Baptist Mission Press. Everyone involved in the trade seemed to know each other. The terrain of print was also a contested one. Many of the writers and printers began as friends but turned rivals, parting ways when ideological differences arose. If we look at some of the seminal works of Rammohun Roy and how they were printed, and under what circumstances, we understand the nature of this terrain. The Baptist Missionary Press published texts that proselytized for Christianity and also printed Rammohun's works that were critical of Christianity. Rammohun was closely attached to the Baptist missionaries, and many of his works on Christianity were printed there. But the Baptist missionaries were not happy with him. This was a bit of a sticky situation as the Baptist Mission press was his publishing house for all the works on the subject of Christianity. Eventually, they refused to publish his works, and in 1823, he printed *The Final Appeal to the Christian Public in Defence of the Precepts of Jesus* which was printed at the Unitarian Press—Rammohun had had to buy his own type and rely on native superintendence.

Debates were made possible through print and they also spilled into the realm of native intellectuals and theologians. Rammohun positioned himself against many of the existing well known *pandits* who were associated with British establishments. Many Indian *pandits*, attached with the Baptist Mission Press, also printed books in Bengali that were of a fictional nature. For example, *Batris Simhasan* was published by Mrityunjar Tarkalankar in 1802. But more importantly, Rammohun was involved in theological debate with Mrityunjay Vidyalankar, who was also the head *pandit* of the government college at Calcutta around 1817. Mrityunjay's *Vedanta Chandrika* (translated into English as *An Apology for the Present System of Hindu Worship)* was critiqued by Rammohun in A *Second Defense of the Monotheistical System of the Veds (Bhattacharyer Sahit Vichar)*. In this realm of print, Rammohun engaged in debate with certain brands of Christianity and Hinduism. There was a blurry line between enemies and friends.

A VINDICATION OF THE INCARNATION OF THE DEITY.[19]

DEDICATION.

TO ALL BELIEVERS IN THE INCARNATION OF THE DEITY.

Fellow Believers,

The following Correspondence between the Renowned Dr. B. Tytler and myself, was partly given to the world through the medium of the *Bengal Harkaru*, but as the Editor of that Paper refused to admit some of my letters into its pages, and those published were widely separated from each other by being mixed up with various extraneous matters, I have deemed it advisable to have the whole collected together and presented at one view, for general edification.

My object in addressing Dr. Tytler (as will be seen from a perusal of the following pages,) was, that all Believers in the Manifestation of God in the flesh, whether Hindoo or Christian, might unite in support of our Common Cause, and cordially co-operate in our endeavours to check the alarming growth of the Unitarian Heresy: but unfortunately my hopes were entirely disappointed; as Dr. Tytler not only refused to repair the breach 1 conceived his writings calculated to make, but to my great surprise and regret, in return for my friendly

---

[19] The full title reads: *A Vindication of the Incarnation of the Deity, as the common basis of Hindooism and Christianity against the schismatic attacks of R. Tytler, Esq., M.D., Surgeon in the Hon. East India Company's Service, ... and also, Member of the Asiatic Society*. By Ram Doss, Calcutta: Printed by S. Smith and Co., Hurkaru Press, 1823.

offers of assistance, he applied to me and to my religion the most opprobrious abuse, and treated me as if my Faith were inimical to the tenets of his Creed.

I am, your Friend and fellow-believer,

Ram Doss,

Calcutta, June 3, 1823.

INTRODUCTION

This Correspondence was occasioned by a passage in a letter of Dr. Tytler's published in the *Bengal Hurkaru* of the 30th of May 1823, directed against Rammohan Roy, a person who, as is well known, is strongly reprobated by the zealous both among Hindoos-and Christians, for his daring impiety in rejecting the doctrine of Divine Incarnations. But the Doctor while censuring this stubborn Heretic most unwarrantably introduced contemptuous allusions to the Hindoo Deities, as will be seen, from the passage referred to which is here subjoined :—

Extract from the Hurkaru —May 3rd, 1823.

He (Rammohun Roy) thus proceeds in the same epistle. "Whether you be a faithful Believer in the Divinity of the Holy Lord and Saviour JESUS CHRIST, or of any other mortal man; or whether a Hindu declares himself a faithful believer in the Divinity of his Holy Thakoor Trata RAM, or MUNOO—I feel equally indifferent about these notions." Here I pause, for the purpose of asking- the candid Reader what, would have been said, if, at the time Rammohan Roy continued in his belief of Siva, Vishnu and Ganesa, I had personally addressed a letter to him, replete with vituperation of him and his opinions? Would it not have been asserted, and very justly, that I was attacking him, and his gods, and wounding the religious feelings of a Hindu? Yet this Unitarian, as he now professes himself, thinks proper to leave the subject of discussion, namely a proposal to hold a "Religious conference" and tells me flatly that my belief in the Divinity of the Holy Saviour is on par with a Hindu's belief in his Thakoor!!! – Yes, Christian Readers, such is the fact; and when I offer to defend myself from such vile imputations by arguments drawn from those Holy Scriptures to which this Unitarian himself appeals, I am given to understand, that this Reviler of my FAITH, the FAITH OF MY ANCESTORS, will not condescend to listen, unless my reply receives the stamp of orthodoxy from the signature of a Missionary!!!

May 2, 1823.

R. Tytler.

RAM DOSS' FIRST LETTER TO DR. TYTLER.

The Editor of the *Hurkaru* having refused insertion to the following, it was privately forwarded to Dr. Tytler.

To, Dr. R. Tytler.

Sir,

I happened to read a Letter in the " Hurkaru" of the 3rd instant, under the signature of R. Tytler, which has excited my wonder and astonishment. For I had heard that you were not only profoundly versed in the knowledge of the ancients, but intimately acquainted with the learning and opinions of the present age. But I felt quite disappointed when I perceived that you entertained ideas so erroneous respecting the Hindoo religion.

Is there any Hindoo who would be offended at being told by a believer in the Invisible God that this man is indifferent about his (the Hindoo's) faith in the divinity of his Holy Thakoor or Trata Ram or Munoo? We know that these selfconceited sects who profess reverence for only one Deity are apt to express their indifference for the holy INCARNATION of the Divine Essence believed in by Hindoos as well as by Christians; and in fact that the followers of any one religion have little respect for the opinions of those of another. But can this give concern or surprise to the enlightened and well-informed persons who have seen and conversed with various sects of men?

I am more particularly astonished that a man of your reputed learning and acquirements, should be offended at the mention of the resemblance of your belief in the Divinity of Jesus Christy with a Hindoo's Belief in his Thakoor; because you ought to know that our religious faith and yours are founded on the same sacred basis, viz, the manifestation of God in the flesh without any restriction to a dark or fair complexion, large or small stature, long or short hair. You cannot surely be ignorant that the Divine Ram was the reputed son of Dasarath, of the offspring of Bhuggeeruth, of the tribe of Rughoo, as Jesus was the reputed son of Joseph, of the House of David of the Tribe of Judah. Ram was the King of the Rughoos and of Foreigners, while in like manner Jesus was King of the Jews and Gentiles. Both are stated in the respective sacred books handed down to us, to have performed very wonderful miracles and both ascended up to Heaven. Both were tempted by the Devil while on the earth, and both have been worshipped by millions up to the present day. Since God can be born of the Tribe of Judah how, I ask, is it impossible that he should be born of the Tribe of Rughoo, or of any other nation or race of men? And as the human form and feelings of Ram afford sceptics no good argument against his omnipresent and divine nature, it must be evident to you that this deluded sect of Unitarianism can lay no stress on the human form and feelings of Jesus Christ as disproving his divinity.

When therefore the resemblance is so very striking, and ought to be known to you as well as to every other man having the least pretensions to an acquaintance with the learning and religion of the Natives of India,—how is it possible that you can feel offended at the mention of a. fact so notorious? Yon may perhaps urge, that there is a wide difference between a belief in three Persons' in the Godhead as maintained by you, and a belief in three hundred and thirty millions of Persons in, the Godhead, entertained by the Hindoos. But as all such numerical objections are founded on the frail basis of human reason, which we well know is fallible, you must admit that the same omnipotence, which can make Three One and One Three, can equally reconcile the unity and Plurality of three hundred and thirty millions; both being supported by a sublime mystery which far transcends all human comprehension.

The vain and narrow-minded Believers in one Invisible God accuse the followers of the Trinity, as well as us the sincere worshippers of Ram and other Divine Incarnations, of being Idolaters; and policy therefore might have suggested to you the propriety of maintaining a good understanding and brotherhood among all who have correct notions of the manifestation of God in the flesh; that we may cordially join and go hand in hand, in opposing and if possible extirpating the abominable notion of a Single God, which strikes equally at the root of Hindooism and Christianity. However, it is not too late for you to reflect on your indiscretion, and atone for it by expressing your regret at having written and published anything calculated to create dissension among the worshippers of Divine Incarnations.

I am, Sir, Your most obedient Servant,

Ram Doss.

DR. TYTLER'S REPLY TO THE FOREGOING.

To Ram Doss,

I have received your letter and beg yon to receive my best thanks, for the trouble you have put yourself to in sending it to me. It was my intent on this evening to have proved that Hindu Idolatry and Unitarianism are the same, and that they both proceed from the Devil.—Unfortunately Mr. Robinson in consequence of the number who were anxious to attend, has requested me to postpone the meeting, to which of course I have acceded. But I am ready,— MIND ME, READY — to meet you and your runnagate friend Rammohun Roy, whenever you please, in public and private discussion, and let you know what a humble individual unsupported can do, armed with no other weapon than the sharp sword of the Gospel, in bringing to light the hidden works of darkness which are at present displayed in the damnable Heresy of Unitariantsm of which you are the wretched tool. But neither you, Rummohun Roy, nor the second fallen ADAM dare meet me because you fear the WORD of TRUTH.

Your inveterate and determined

foe in the LORD.
May Gift, 1823. (Signed) R. TYTLER.

RAM DOSS'S REPLY TO A REMARK OF THE EDITOR OF THE *BENGAL HURKARU.*

Sir,

To the Editor of the *Bengal Hurkaru,*

After publishing in your Paper of the 3rd instant Dr. Tytler's letter throwing out offensive insinuations against the Hindu Religion as unworthy to be compared with the Christian, I am truly astonished at your refusal to insert my very friendly Reply and expostulation with him for the error and indiscretion into which he has fallen, and that you moreover defend him in the following words: "We would hint to Ram Doss that there is in our opinion a wide difference between the belief which maintains God to have appeared in the Flesh and that of the Hindoo who believes the appearance of the omnipotent Being in the shape of a Thakoor, which if we "are not mistaken, is composed of stone, metal or wood."

I must remark, first, on the total unacquaintance, you have displayed, with the Hindoo Religion, notwithstanding your residence in the capital of Bengal, in which however you are more excusable than Dr. Tytler, considering his high pretensions to learning. Can you find a single Hindoo in the whole of India, who imagines that the divine Ram, the son of Dusruth by Koushilya his mother according to the flesh, was composed either of wood, stone or metal? If you can find even one, there may be some excuse for your mistake in supposing, what is so wide of the fact.—You may of course find numerous consecrated images or statues of the Holy Ram, in the Hindu temples, formed of wood and other materials, placed there for the pious purpose of attracting the attention of Devotees to that Divine Incarnation ;— although many good Hindoos do not consider such representations as necessary, and worship Ram directly without the intervention of any sensible object. But can you suppose for a moment that a model or picture o any person, whether divine or human, can identify that being with such representation or convert the original existence into the same materials? If this were the case, then the number of men so unfortunate as to have statues or portraits of themselves made, must lose their real essence—their original elements necessarily degenerating into stone, or paint and canvass.

But it is indisputable that neither the image of the Holy Jesus in Roman Catholic Churches, nor the representations of the Divine Ram in the Hindu Temples, are identified with either of those sacred persons.

As you have refused to publish my letter in answer to Dr. Tytler's attack, I shall take an opportunity of sending it directly to himself for his consideration and reply, and purpose very soon laying this controversy before the public through some other channel with proper mention of your partial conduct, in circulating Dr. Tytler's insulting insinuations against the Hindu Religion and withholding my answer thereto for its vindication. 1 expect you will kindly insert this letter in your Paper of tomorrow along with a justification of your own observations of this morning.

I am, Sir, your most obedient Servant,

Ram Doss.

REMARKS OF THE EDITOR RELATIVE OT THE FOREGOING

(Contained in the Bengal Hurkaru of the 8th May.)

In our subsequent pages will be found a letter signed Ram Doss, which we insert with pleasure, with a desire of convincing him that we are really impartial in our views of the subject of which it treats. In explanation of our refusal to insert the former letter of Ram Doss, we owe it to him to say that although it justly deserves, the appellation of a " very friendly reply" and although it was written with much ability, yet it appeared to us to overstep the limits we have prescribed to ourselves, by entering too far into the subject of the original dispute between the two classes of religious professors, instead of being confined to the discussion of the subject between Rammohun Roy and Dr. Tytler, namely the right of the latter to demand, and of the former to afford, facilities for the purpose of the discussion of the point at issue between them. It was under these circumstances and with this feeling that we are declined to insert Ram Doss's communication, and we beg to assure him that it was not from any disrespect to him, or partiality for Dr. Tytler or his doctrines.

Having disposed of this part of the subject we trust to the satisfaction of Ram Doss we shall simply remark on the other, that we never intended to Intimate that any sensible Hindoo could for one moment suppose that God was personally present in an image of brass, stone or metal; but we have no hesitation in asserting that such an opinion does prevail, not only among the Hindoos, but amongst the ignorant of all classes whose religious faith prescribes the worship of images as the medium of access to the Deity. We really ought not to enter on the discussion of any of the points connected with the religious worship of the Hindoos, as we have had but very few opportunities of making ourselves acquainted with them, and if we are now in any error on these subjects, we trust that Ram Doss will attribute it to the causes which we have thus explained, and not to any feeling of partiality towards Dr. Tytler, or of misrepresentation of the objects of his own worship.

RAM DOSS' FIRST CHALLENGE TO Dr. R. TYTLER,

To the Editor of the Bengal Hurkatu.

Sir,

Being disappointed in my just expectation of. having my answer to Dr. Tytler's insinuations inserted in your Paper, I yesterday sent it to the Doctor himself for his consideration; but he avoids making a reply thereto, and in answer to my arguments merely returns abuse against me, and likewise against our common enemies, the Unitarians, for which last I of course care nothing.

I take this opportunity of informing the Public that this Goliath, notwithstanding his high pretensions to learning, and presumption in setting himself up as the champion of Christianity, shrinks from the defence of the charges he has brought against Hindooism, and that he refuses to co-operate with me in opposing Unitarianism, although, he declares in his note to me - that it is a system of damnable heresy proceeding from the Devil.

I am, Sir, Your obedient Servant.

May 7, 1823.

Ram Doss.

DR. TYTLER'3 REPLY TO RAM DOSS

To the Editor of the Bengal Hurkaru.

As I do not intend this letter to have any direct reference, to the subject of Religious discussion, you will oblige me by giving it insertion into the columns of the Hurkaru. Two day ago I received an Epistle subscribed Ram Doss which I was led to conclude must have been written by some Unitarian under a pseudonymous signature. But it appears from a letter, which is published in your paper of this day, l may have been mistaken; and I am, therefore, anxious to inform Ram Doss, if he be a real person, that I consider there is no book at present in possession of *Hindus,*—the *Mahabharat* and *Ramayuna* not excepted,—of higher antiquity than the entrance of the Mussulmans into-India,? say about 800 years from the present period. The legends attached to the *Avatars* are merely perverted, and corrupted copies of the Holy Scriptures in the possession of Christians, and have no particular relation to the ancient religion, whatever it may have been, of the inhabitants of this country. Should Ram Doss therefore be a real person, and wish to obtain information on those topics, it will afford me sincere pleasure to meet him, either at my own house or any other he may appoint, at some hour convenient to us both, for the purpose of explaining the arguments, which support the views I have taken of the *Modernness* of the religious system at, present followed by the Hindus.

Your obedient Servant,

May 8, 1833.

R. Tytler.

R.AM DOSS'S SECOND CHALLENGE TO DR. TYTLER.

To the Editor of the Bengal Hurkaru,

Sir,

Dr. Tytler having been unable to make a direct reply to the arguments conveyed in my letter to him dated the 5th instant, has taken refuge in your Paper, knowing very well that, he would prevail upon you to insert every assertion that he might make against our Sacred Books and Holy incarnations, and that you as a Christian would excuse yourself for declining to give publicity to my retaliation, upon him.

I therefore challenge him through your Pages for a reply to my arguments in the shape of a letter, so that I may endeavour through some other means to publish all our correspondence for the consideration and judgment of the Public.

I am, Sir, your obedient Servant,

9th May, 1823.

Ram Doss.

DR. TYTLER'S REPLY TO RAM DOSS.

To the Editor of the Bengal Hurkaru.

Sir,

Your Correspondent Ram Doss in "informing the public" that I consider Unitarianism as a system of damnable heresy proceeding from the Devil" has forgot to mention that such was also my expressed opinion to him respecting the superstitions to which he is so extremely partial. Under those circumstances is it reasonable to expect, I will allow him to cooperate with me, as he calls it, "against our common enemies," when in fact I maintain *Unitarianism* to be nothing more than a new name for Hindoo Idolatry.

Your Obedient Servant,

Calcutta, May 10, 1823.

R. Tytler.

RAM DOSS' THIRD CHALLENGE TO DR. TYTLER

To the Editor of the Bengal Hurkaru.

Sir,

One of the objects of my Letter to Dr. Tytler, was to solicit the co-operation of the Doctor in opposing Unitarians. The other, to refute his insinuations against Hindooism and, prove that it was founded on the same sacred basis (the Manifestation of God in the flesh) with Doctor Tytler's own Faith.

From the Doctors letter in your paper of this morning, I see he positively shrinks from entering the field with me against Unitarianism, leaving me thus to encounter the danger and reap the glory single-handed.

I now request to be informed through the medium of your paper, whether the *Doctor* also flinches from justifying his insinuations against the Hindoo Religion, and replying to my letter proving Hindooism and Christianity to rest on the same sacred foundation.

I am, Sir,

Your obedt. Servt.

May 12th, 1823.

Ram Doss.

DR. TYTLER'S REPLY TO RAM DOSS.

To the Editor of the Bengal Hurkaru. .

Sir,

The assertion of Ram Doss that "I shrink from entering the field against Unitarianism, leaving him thus to encounter, the danger and reap the glory single handed," when all Calcuttta is acquainted with the contrary, and no one better than the Unitarians themselves, is really too absurd to require notice.

In support of what this writer calls "my Insinuations against the Hindoo Religion," I refer him to the histories of *Buddha, Suluvahuna,* and *Chrishna,* and maintain they comprise nothing more than perverted copies of Christianity. Let him show the reverse if he can.

Your Obedient Servant,

Calcutta, May 13, 1823.

R. Tytler.

RAM DOSS'S REPLY TO THE FOREGOING.

To the Editor of the Bengal Hurkaru,

Sir,

You are aware that I have three times through the medium of your paper, called upon Dr. Tytler, to reply to the Arguments contained in the letter, forwarded to him by me and the receipt of which he acknowledged in a *torrent of abuse* and that he has as often as thus publicly called upon, returned an evasive answer, which proves that he inwardly shrinks from the combat.

With a view to defend his Offensive insinuations, against Hindooism, he now refers me to the Histories of Buddha (the head of a tribe inimical to Hindooism) Sulavahana (an Indian Prince) and Chrishna, a *divine Incarnation* without attempting to bring forward from these any thing against the justness of my arguments—I now, Sir, beg leave to appeal to you, whether if any Hindoo were to make insinuations against the Christian Religion, when called to defend them he would be justified in merely referring Christians to the Books of the Jews (a tribe equally in inimical to Christianity) or Gibbon's *History of the Roman Empire* or to a whole History of Jesus Christ, without adducing any particular Passage? I now for the Fourth and last time call upon the *Doctor,* either to answer precisely my arguments already in his possession, or confess publicly that he is totally unable to justify his insinuations against a Religion founded on the Sacred basis of the manifestation of God in the flesh, and that knowing the badness of his cause, he shrinks from meeting me on the fair field of *Regular Argument,* instead of which he has given me only abuse.

I have nothing to say respecting his mode of opposing our Common enemies the Unitarians, and grant him freely the honour of his individual exertions. Notwithstanding I think it is proper to suggest the expediency of Common believers in Divine incarnations (like the Doctor and myself) joining hand in hand in opposing our inveterate enemy. Our chance of success must be greater when our Force is united, than when it is divided.

I am, Sir, Your obedient Servant.

Ram Doss.

May 14th, 1823.

DR. TYTLER'S REPLY TO RAM DOSS.

This Reply was in a Postscript to a Letter of Dr. Tytler (dated May 15,) addressed to the Editor of the *Bengal Harkaru* and published in that Paper of the 16th May.

"I request" (said the Doctor) "to be informed by your sapient correspondent Ram Doss, in what manner he proves *Buddha* to be 'the head of a tribe' inimical to Hindooism."

RAM DOSS' REPLY TO THE FOREGOING.

To the Editor of the Bengal Hurkaru.

Sir,

The only reply which Dr. Tytler makes to my Fourth Challenge published in your paper yesterday is as follows viz. -

P. S. I request to be informed by our sapient correspondent Ram Doss in what manner he proves Buddha to "be the head of a tribe inimical to Hindooism"?

I now call on the Public to pronounce whether this query can be considered as a reply to the arguments contained in my letter forwarded to the Doctor, repelling his offensive insinuations and proving that Hindooism and Christianity are founded on the same basis? or if it be not evidently a mere pretence for evading the question? Fully warranted in anticipating a verdict in my favor, I ask what opinion will the world form of a man who with some pretensions to learning and great professions of Religion, while defying the whole world in the field of Religious discussion, first utters degrading Insinuations against a Faith founded on exactly the same basis as his own, and then when repeatedly challenged to justify this conduct resorts to such *Shuffling* and *Evasion?* — However to oblige the Doctor as a fellow-believer in, and worshipper of Divine Incarnations, I will inform him (although it has no bearing on the question) that *Buddha* or *Booddha,* is the head of the sect of *Bauddhas,* who derive their name from him in the same manner as Christians do from Christ. That this sect is inimical to Hindooism is proved by the fact that they deny the existence of a Creator of the Universe, in whom the Hindoos believe, and also despise many of the Gods worshipped by the latter. There are hundreds of works published by them against each other which are in general circulation. But all this has nothing to with my arguments which the Doctor by evading virtually confesses he is unable to answer. I therefore denounce him a defamer of Hindooism, a religion of the principles of which he is (or at least appears to be) totally ignorant.

I am, Sir, your obedient servant,

Ram Doss.

Friday, 16th May, 1823.

DR. TYTLER'S REPLY TO THE FOREGOING.

Published in the *Harkaru* of May 22nd.

The sapient Ram Doss now changes his tone,—and tells us the *Buddhists* "despise many of the Gods worshipped by the Hindoos." It hence follows that *some* of the Hindoo deities must be objects of their adoration. And yet this writer asserts *Buddha* to be the " head of a tribe inimical to Hindoism "while his own statement proves Hindoo Gods to be the objects of *Buddhaic* veneration !!.

RAM DOSS' REPLY TO THE FOREGOING.

To the Editor of the Bengal Hurkaru,

In your paper of this day, Dr. Tytler notices my fifth challenge, calling upon him to answer the arguments contained in my letter forwarded to him some weeks ago, repelling his offensive insinuations against Hindooism — But how does he justify himself? "The sapient Ram Doss" (says he) "now changes his tone and tells us "the Buddhists despise many *of* the Gods worshipped by the Hindoos." It hence follows that *some* of the Hindoo deities must be objects of their adoration—And yet this writer asserts Buddha to be the head of a tribe inimical to Hindooism, while his own statement proves Hindoo Gods to be the objects of Buddhaic veneration.

I now beg to call the attention of the Public, Christians and not Christians to the above passage, and request them to pronounce whether the Doctor thereby proves that Hindooism cannot (as insinuated) be compared with Christianity, or refutes my position, that these two religious are founded on the same sacred basis, viz the Manifestation of God in the Flesh? and I now call on the world to judge, whether the person who can resort to such shuffling and evasion have any just claim to the character of a man of learning, or a man of probity? –What name is bestowed on the man who thus shrinks from meeting the arguments of his opponent fairly and candidly, and trembling at the force of truth, is glad to make his escape by any mean subterfuge?

It is almost self-degradation or a prostitution of reason to treat his last remark, above-quoted, as worthy of notice, viz- that as "Buddhists despise many of the Gods worshipped by the Hindoos, it hence follows that *some* of the Hindoo deities Must be subjects of their "adoration." *Indeed!* In what school of wisdom did the learned Doctor acquire his Logic? Although I *despise* or dislike several members of a family, is this a proof that I must adore the rest? May I not regard the rest with indifference, or be unacquainted with them? But granting even that Buddhists do worship *some* of the Hindoo Gods, while they despise others, may they not still be inimical *to* Hindooism? For, don't the Jews despise one of the Christian God's, worship another, and are indifferent to a third; and yet are they not inveterate enemies of Christianity?

I now only wish to know from what College or University the Doctor procured a Certificate, authorizing him to assume the Title of *M. D.* and whether that seat of Learning in the distribution of its *Academic Honors usually* selects such worthy subjects?

I am, Sir, Your obedient Servant.

Ram Doss.

Thursday, 22nd May 1823.

P. S. I congratulate the Doctor On his Victory (as reported by himself in your paper of today) over our common enemies the Unitarians (these deluded deniers of Divine Incarnation), and I regret I was present to share in the triumph. - R. D.

Dr. Tytler being now, it appears, completely silenced, a Friend under the signature of A Christian, came forward to his assistance in the following Letter.

LETTER OF A CHRISTIAN TO RAM DOSS

To the Editor of the Bengal Hurkaru,

It is gratifying to the lovers of science to behold a few intelligent Hindoos emerging from the degraded ignorance and shameful superstition in which their fathers for so many centuries have been buried. It is no less pleasing to the friends of humanity, to find that one of the most learned of the Hindoo Brahmins has not only abandoned the doctrine which countenances the cruel and abominable practice of matricide, but also ably confuted his compeers, who were advocates for having human victims sacrificed to Moloch.

On the other hand it is a sad contemplation, that these very individuals who are indebted to Christians for the civil liberty they enjoy, as well as for the rays of intelligence now beginning to dawn on them, should in the most ungenerous manner insult their benefactors by endeavouring to degrade their religion, for no other reason, but because they cannot comprehend its sublime Mysteries.

My attention has been particularly attracted to this subject by a letter signed Ram Doss which appeared in your paper of yesterday.

This Hindoo with whom I have no personal acquaintance had the arrogance to lay before the public the following passage "I now call on the *public* to pronounce whether this query can be considered as a reply to the arguments contained in my letter forwarded to the Doctor, repelling his offensive insinuations and proving that *Hindooism and Christianity* are founded on the same basis?" Ram Doss here appeals to the public, and he will ofcourse grant me the same privilege. I will therefore ask,— Christian Readers, are you so far degraded by Asiatic effeminacy as to behold with indifference your holy and immaculate

Religion thus degraded by having it placed on an equality with Hindooism—with rank idolatry— with disgraceful ignorance and shameful superstition?

Will Ram Doss or his associates be pleased to inform me, if the *Incarnation of his God* was foretold by Prophets through a period of four thousand years? Or will he demonstrate the mission or divine incarnation of his *Deity* by incontestable and stupendous miracles such as Christ wrought? Will he assert that the doctrine of Hindooism is as pure and undefiled as that of Christianity? Or in fine will he prove that the human character has ever been exalted by any religious system so much as by the sweet influence of Christianity?

If Ram Doss is not able satisfactorily to clear up a single point of what I now submit to his serious consideration, it is manifest, that in common civility, he should refrain from insulting Christians by putting their religion on a comparison with Hindooism.

Rammohun Roy, who appears to me to be the most learned of the Hindoos, is so far from making such odious and offensive remarks, that he apparently gives the preference to Christianity. Vide, his First Appeal entitled "the precepts of Christ the guide to peace and happiness." I regret the learned Brahmin was interrupted by the intemperate zeal of the Baptists the praise-worthy course he intended to have pursued as set forth in his preface to the work above alluded to.

I conclude by recommending your sapient Correspondent Ram Doss to employ his time and talents in laudable and pious endeavors to reclaim his Countrymen from idolatory, rather than to investigate mysteries that are far above the weak comprehensions of man. I also recommend him to beware of such Christians as are carried away with every wind of doctrine, and who know not what they do.

1 am, Sir, your Obedient Servant,

A Christian.

RAM DOSS' REPLY TO THE CHRISTIAN.

[Published in a Pamphlet containing an account of Dr. Tytler's Lecture circulated with the Bengal Hurkaru Newspaper.]

Sir,

To the Editor of the Bengal Hurkaru.

I regret to observe by the Letter in your Paper of this morning signed A Christian that in repelling the offensive insinuations of Dr. Tytler against the Hindoo Religion, I am considered by one of the Christian denomination as endeavouring to degrade his *faith*.

It is well known to you, Sir, that I privately sent a Letter to the Doctor, refuting his position in the most friendly, calm, and argumentative manner, to which he returned a note loading me with the grossest abuse; consequently I thought myself justified in challenging him publicly to make a reply to my arguments. The Christian therefore cannot conceal from himself that it is *I* and *my* Faith which have been vilified and abused, and that in return I have offered *not* insult, but merely reason and argument; for it cannot be considered insult for a man to say that another religion is founded on the same basis with his own, which he believes to be all that is venerable and sacred.

If by the "Ray of Intelligence" for which the Christian says we are indebted to the English, he means the introduction of useful mechanical arts, I am ready to express my assent and also my gratitude; but with respect to *Science, Literature or Religion,* I do not acknowledge that we are placed under any obligation. For by a reference to history it may be proved that the World was indebted to *our ancestors* for the first dawn of knowledge, which sprung up in the East, and thanks to the Goddess of Wisdom, we have still a philosophical and copious language of our own which distinguishes us from other nations, who cannot express scientific or abstract ideas without borrowing the language of foreigners.

Rammohun Roy's abandonment of Hindoo doctrines (as "A Christian" mentions) cannot prove them to be erroneous; no more than the rejections of the Christian Religion by hundreds of persons who were originally Christians and more learned than Rammohun Roy, proves the fallacy of Christianity. We

Hindoos regard him in the same light a Christians do Hume, Voltaire, Gibbon and other Sceptics.

Before "A Christian" indulged in a tirade about person's being "degraded by *Asiatic* effeminacy" he should have recollected that almost all the ancient prophets and. patriarchs venerated by Christians, nay even Jesus Christ himself, a Divine Incarnation and the *founder* of the Christian Faith, were ASIATICS, so that if a Christian thinks it degrading to be born or to reside in *Asia,* he directly reflects upon them.

First—The *Christian* demands "Will Ram Doss or his associates be pleased to inform me if the *Incarnation of his God* was foretold by Prophets through a period of four thousand years?" I answer in the affirmative. The Incarnation of Ram was foretold in the works of many holy and inspired men for more than 4000 years previous to the event, in the most precise and intelligible language; not in those ambiguous and equivocal terms found in the *Old Testament,* respecting the Incarnation of Jesus Christ, an ambiguity which it is well known has afforded our common enemies the Unitarians a handle for raising a doubt of Jesus Christ being a real Manifestation of God in the flesh. " . '

Secondly—The Christian demands of Ram Doss "Will he demonstrate the mission or divine incarnation of his deity by incontestable and Stupendous Miracles such as Christ wrought?" I answer, Yes: The divine Ram performed miracles more stupendous, not before multitudes of ignorant people only, but in the presence of Princes and of thousands of learned men, and of those who were inimical to Hindooism. I admit that the Jains and other unbelievers ascribed Ram's miraculous power to a Demoniacal Spirit, in the same manner as the Jews attributed the miracles of Jesus to the power of Beelzebub; but neither of these objections are worthy of notice from believers in Divine Incarnations; since the performance of the miracles themselves is incontestably proved, by tradition.

Thirdly,—The Christian asks, "Will he (Ram Doss) assert that the Doctrine of Hindooism is as pure and undefiled as that of Christianity?" Undoubtedly, such is my assertion: and an English translation of the Vedant as well as of Munoo (which contains the essences of the whole Veds) being before the public, I call on reflecting men to compare the two religions together, and point out in what respect the one excels the other in purity? Should the Christian attempt to ridicule some part of the ritual of the Veds I shall of course feel myself justified in referring to ceremonies of a similar character in the Christian Scriptures; and if he dwell on the corrupt notions introduced into Hindooism in more modern times, I shall also remind him of the corruptions introduced by various sects into Christianity. But A *Christian* must know very well that such corruptions cannot detract from the excellence of Genuine Religions themselves.

Fourthly.—The Christian asks, "Will he (Ram Doss) prove that the human character has ever been exalted by any system of religion so much as by the sweet influence of Christianity." In reply, I appeal to History, and call upon the Christian to mention any religion on the face of the earth that has been the cause of so much war and bloodshed, cruelty and oppression for so many hundred years as this whose *"sweet influence"* he celebrates.

That propriety of conduct found among the better sort of Christians is entirely owing to the superior education they have enjoyed; a proof of which is, that others of the same rank in society, although not believers in Christianity are distinguished by equal propriety of conduct, which is not the case with the most firm believers, if destitute of Education or without the means of improvement by mixing in company with persons better instructed than themselves.

It is unjust is the Christian to quarrel with Hindoos because (he says) they cannot comprehend the sublime mystery of his Religion; since he is equally unable to comprehend the sublime mysteries of ours, and since, both these mysteries equally transcend the human understanding, one cannot be preferred to the other.

Let us however return to the main question, viz. that THE INCARNATION OF THE DEITY IS THE COMMON BASIS OF HINDOOISM AND CHRISTIANITY. If the manifestation of God in the flesh is possible such possibility cannot reasonably be confined to Judea or Ayodhya, for God has undoubtedly the power of manifesting himself in either country, and of assuming any colour or name he pleases. If it is impossible, as our common enemies the Unitarians contend, such impossibility must extend to all places and persons. I trust therefore the Christian will reflect with great seriousness on this subject and will be kind enough to let me know the result.

I am, Sir, your most Obedient Servant,

Ram Doss.

Calcutta, May 23,1823.

Ram Doss having heard nothing more publicly or privately from Dr. Tytler or "A Christian" the correspondence here concluded, and the arguments adduced in vindication of the Incarnation of the Deity as the Common Basis of Hindooism and Christianity consequently remain unanswered.

FINIS.

6 CONCLUSION: JEREMY BENTHAM AND RAMMOHUN ROY.

I conclude by referring to a letter that Jeremy Bentham wrote to Rammohun in 1831,[20] where Bentham describes himself as having had a great influence on James Mill who dictated the histories of India through his work, *The History of British India* (1818); Mill is seen as a family friend, a discipline and a student of Bentham. What is of immense interest is how Bentham subtly suggests to Rammohun that his ideas have been influential in determining the future of India, via the various people whom he knew (he mentions many officials of the EIC and James Mill, of course) and therefore, his establishment of the new penal system in England—the panopticon—is also an institution that Rammohun could consider for India. Bentham wrote, requesting Rammohun to join in the process of establishing an ideal prison system in India:

> What say you to the making singly or in conjunction with other enlightened philanthropists, an offer to Government for that purpose [of building the panopticon]? Professors of all religion might join the contract; and appropriate

[20] Letter from Jeremy Bentham to Rammohun Roy" in Sophia Dobson Collet, *The Life and Letters of Raja Rammohun Roy*, ed. Dilip Kumar Biswas and Prabhat Chandra Ganguli. (Calcutta: Sadharon Brahmo Samaj, 1900). Reprint 1988, pp.452-456.

classification and separation for the persons under management provision correspondent to their several religions, and their respective castes; or other allocations under their respective religions.[21]

This is a fascinating anecdote to narrate, showing us the near macabre ways in which the new modern systems of knowledge that were emerging in the West were transferred to the colonies; Bentham suggests that the bodies of the native inmates would be classified and separated according to their religions and castes and a new panoptical system could be established in India. According to Michel Foucault, the panopticon's method of classifying and codifying was a perfect example of the new forms of knowledge systems that emerged in the eighteenth and nineteenth centuries where knowledge was intrinsically connected with power.[22] Foucault describes how the eighteenth- to nineteenth-century transformation of the human sciences was "set in the context of practices of discipline, surveillance, and constraint, which made possible new kinds of knowledge of human beings even as they created new forms of social control."[23] The new systems of human sciences allowed for greater knowledge about the self, but simultaneously, made it inevitable that the body would be under greater control. State

---

[21] Ibid., p. 456.

[22] Michel Foucault, *Discipline and Punishment. The Birth of a Prison.* (New York: Vintage, 1995). Also see Michel Foucault, *The History of Sexuality, Vol. I* .(New York: Vintage, 1990).

[23] Joseph Rouse, "Power and Knowledge," in *The Cambridge Companion to Foucault*, ed. Gary Gutting (Cambridge: Cambridge University Press, 2006), pp. 95-122.

sponsored surveillance and discipline of the body produced "docile" bodies; as Foucault wrote:

> The human body was entering a machinery of power that explores it, breaks it down and rearranges it. . . . It defined how one may have a hold over others' bodies, not only so that they may do what one wishes, but so that they may operate as one wishes, with the techniques, the speed and the efficiency that one determines. Thus discipline produces subjected and practiced bodies, "docile" bodies.[24]

Bentham's prison system was one such institution which, through its method of control and surveillance of the inmates, was meant to create reformed bodies. The letter that Bentham wrote to Rammohun indicates that the structural changes that were taking place in the eighteenth and the nineteenth centuries, were in the process of being transferred to the colonies. In the colonies, though, the very nature of colonial power itself underwent transformation; the printed book had the power to change the native social structures. The natives took print culture and used it for their means. The transference of western modernity through these figures and print is a subject that needs to be examined at further lengths.

---

[24] Michel Foucault, *Discipline and Punishment*, p. 138.

ABOUT THE AUTHOR

O₂pen Windows: A Feminist Resource and Research Center.

O₂pen Windows is a feminist research cum *adda* center, based in Bangalore. If it could, it would sustain itself with endless cups of tea and lots of stimulating research.

The Purpose: O₂pen Windows encourages research on both contemporary and historical socio-cultural issues and literary issues. These findings will subsequently be documented, archived and published as monographs and essays.

For more information, write to: openwindows101@gmail.com.

VISIT US AT: www.aresourcecenter.wordpress.com.

www.ingramcontent.com/pod-product-compliance
Lightning Source LLC
Chambersburg PA
CBHW071841020426

42331CB00007B/1817